THE LITTLE BOOK OF
ALGORITHMS
2.0

ISBN: 978-1-9161163-4-4

For the latest free download of this book, go to http://bit.do/LBOA2

Email feedback and corrections to the author: william.lau@computingatschool.org.uk

Twitter: @MrLauLearning

I dedicate this book to my colleagues and students at Central Foundation Boys' School. You have to be brave to choose (to teach or learn) computer science; it is not easy and it is not for the faint- hearted!

To Lloyd, Leila, Jaime, Gavin and the brave computer science students at CFBS - this is for you

CONTENTS

Preface.. 3

1. If Statements: Lowest number............................ 7
2. String slicing and concatenation........................ 17
3. Area of a circle....................................... 21
4. Modulo: Odd or even.................................... 25
5. For Loops... 29
6. While Loops... 30
7. Unlimited pin attempts................................. 31
8. Basic login system.................................... 32
9. Lowest number in a list............................... 37
10. Linear search... 38
11. Total of a list....................................... 49
12. Linear search in a 2D list............................ 53
13. Total of a 2D list.................................... 57
14. Login system by reading a file....................... 65
15. Writing a list to a file............................. 69
16. Adding to a list in a file........................... 70
17. Converting binary to denary.......................... 75
18. Converting denary to binary.......................... 76
19. Solutions.. 89
20. Further reading...................................... 116
21. Acknowledgements..................................... 118
22. Space for further practise and notes................. 119

PREFACE

This book is designed to help teachers and students build fluency in their Python programming. It is aimed at students who have already been introduced to the three basic programming constructs of structured programming, namely sequence, selection and iteration. The original aim was to help my Year 11 students with their GCSE Computer Science programming exam. However I hope many students and teachers will find this book useful. The algorithms are represented using Python as this is a popular language with a low threshold for learning.

I was inspired to write this book after reading articles by Scott Portnoff, Sue Sentance and Richard Pawson; three luminaries in the world of computer science education. All three have made me ask the question,

"Why is learning programming so difficult?"

Like many readers, I too found programming challenging and I am *still* learning! After teaching programming for the past seven years, I noticed that only a minority of my students felt confident enough to program independently after two years of instruction. Upon realising this, I knew I had to change my pedagogy.

I believe Scott Portnoff is correct; students do need to memorise some key programming constructs e.g. if statements, while loops and for loops. This will decrease cognitive load and enable students to practise more fluently. Portnoff's work was my starting point for this book. As a student of b-boy and hip-hop culture, I came across Joseph Schloss's book *Foundation* where he writes about a *musical* canon that exists for b-boys. To add to this theory, Jonathan Sacks argues that a *literary* canon is essential to a culture. In linking these three ideas together, I thought about creating a canon for programmers. Perhaps there is a set of programs which represent algorithms that every computer science student should familiarise themselves with?

I started to compile a list of programs based on my experience as a teacher and examiner. Many of the shorter programs are worth repeating until they are committed to memory and I admit that learning some of the longer programs by heart is both challenging and futile. Therefore, to help you develop fluency, I have also written some challenges based on this canon. These challenges should help you understand these programs by applying them.

Sue Sentance suggested in her introduction to programming courses, that we should introduce students to subroutines in their very first program. Richard Pawson goes one step further in edition 07 of the *Hello World* magazine; here Pawson puts forward a case for teaching using the functional programming (FP) paradigm from the outset. He makes a strong case for using functions which return values rather than containing inputs and outputs. This seems counterintuitive due to the perceived complexity of FP syntax, however there are three key arguments for using functions- unit testing of individual functions, code reusability, and a separation of concerns. I would therefore encourage readers to write with functions from the very beginning. This seems daunting at first, however repetition will lead to fluency.

Despite the irrefutable advantages of FP, I have to be pragmatic and will include procedures (subroutines which do not return values) and also programs which do not use subroutines at all. Whilst, I recognise this might be a step away from the FP paradigm; students are likely to encounter simple imperative programming questions up to at least GCSE level. Not including examples of both imperative programming and FP paradigms would be doing our students a disservice. For some algorithms, the exclusion of functions also reduces complexity and cognitive load therefore providing a shallower learning curve.

In order to keep programs as short as possible and to improve readability, comments are not generally provided in the programs. Instead, a more detailed explanation is explained below each program. In lessons, I have found it useful to go through one or two algorithms at the front of the book with my students and then go on to apply this to the associated challenges. Alternatively, students may choose to work through the book independently in class or at home.

This book will hopefully help you to practise and develop fluency in your programming. Learning programming is similar to learning a musical instrument. Both involve practise and making lots of mistakes. Both also require perseverance to develop fluency. Keep going!

WHAT'S NEW IN VERSION 2.0?

Teaching, like software development and learning is about refinement. In this new version there are two key changes.

Firstly, challenges now directly follow each relevant skill. This reflects the structure of most mathematics textbooks and workbooks. It means there's less time and effort spent flicking backwards and forwards.

Secondly, there are a greater number and range of challenges because you will become a better programmer and computer scientist by solving a greater number and range of problems.

While answers remain in the back of the book, I have also started creating walkthrough video solutions to some of the more complex challenges. These are available on Youtube at: https://bit.do/LBOAVids

I wish you the very best on your learning journey.

LOWEST NUMBER

A program which takes two numbers as inputs and outputs the smallest number.

When you first started programming, you may have produced a program to ouput a lower number without using subroutines.

```
1   num1 = int(input("Enter the first number: "))
2   num2 = int(input("Enter the second number: "))
3
4   if num1 <= num2:
5       lowest = num1
6   else:
7       lowest = num2
8
9   print("The lowest number is " + str(lowest))
```

You may even be asked to write simple programs like this in your exams. However, good programmers write code which can be reused and tested in isolation (known as unit testing). Therefore, using a subroutine (also known as a subprogram) to create a procedure would produce a "better" program that is modular:

```
1   def lower_num(num1,num2):
2       if num1 <= num2:
3           lowest = num1
4       else:
5           lowest = num2
6
7       print("The lowest number is " + str(lowest))
8
9
10  first_num = int(input("Enter the first number: "))
11  second_num = int(input("Enter the second number: "))
12
13  lower_num(first_num,second_num)
```

Whilst the use of a procedure in the second program allows you to call the subprogram multiple times in the main program, it does not allow for full code re-use...

LOWEST NUMBER CONTINUED...

...What happens if you wanted to use this lowest number later in the program? In this case, it makes sense to use a function. The key difference is that functions return values whereas procedures do not.

```
1   def lower_num(num1,num2):
2       if num1 <= num2:
3           return num1
4       else:
5           return num2
6
7
8   first_num = int(input("Enter the first number: "))
9   second_num = int(input("Enter the second number: "))
10
11  lowest = lower_num(first_num,second_num)
12
13  print("The lowest number is " + str(lowest))
```

- The function `lower_num` is defined on lines 1-5. We have to define functions before we can call (use) them.
- Usage of the function is demonstrated on lines 8-13. We still take two numbers as integer inputs on Lines 8-9.
- Line 11 calls the function `lower_num` with two arguments: the contents of `first_num` and `second_num variables`. These arguments are passed into the parameters num1 and num2 respectively[1]. The result is stored in the variable `lowest`.
- As the returned value is an integer, it is cast to a string on line 13 using str(lowest) so that it can be concatenated (the technical name for joining text) with the meaningful output message.

[1] Arguments and parameters should have different names even if they seem to serve the same purpose. In this case both num1 and first_num store the first number. However, the argument stored in the variable `first_num` has global scope, it can be accessed and changed anywhere in the program. The parameter num1 has local scope, it is a local variable which can only be accessed in the subroutine.

CHALLENGE 1: HIGHEST NUMBER

Write a subprogram that has three parameters, num1, num2 and num3. The program should take three numbers as arguments and return the highest number.

```
def highest_number(num1, num2, num3):
    if num1 >= num2 and num1 >= num3:
```

CHALLENGE 2: CALLING HIGHEST NUMBER

Complete the program below which asks the user to enter three integers and then calls the `highest_number` subprogram from the previous page. The returned value is stored in a variable called `highest` and then output as a meaningful message

```
num1_in = int(input("Enter the first number"))

num2_in = int(input("Enter the second number"))



_____


highest = highest_number(                        )


print("The highest number was                    )
```

CHALLENGE 3: OPTIONS

Complete the subprogram below. The subprogram has a parameter called `num` which takes a number as an argument and returns a subject. These numbers correspond to the following subjects:

1 Computer Science
2 Music
3 Dance
4 PE

If the student passes any other value into num, it should return "Error"

```
def options(            ):
        if num == 1:
            return "Computer Science"
        elif num == 2:
            return "Music"
```

11

CHALLENGE 4: CALLING OPTIONS

Write a program which calls the subprogram `options` from Challenge 3. A user should be prompted to enter a number to choose a GCSE option. The program should then output a meaningful confirmation message based on the user's input.

CHALLENGE 5: TRACING IF STATEMENTS

Q1) State the output for the following program when the program is run four times with four different inputs:

num_in	Ouput
8	8
3	
12	
5	

```
1    def mystery_number(num):
2        if num < 5:
3            print(8)
4        elif num < 3:
5            print(8)
6        elif num == 3:
7            print(3)
8        else:
9            print(num)
10
11   num_in = int(input("Enter a number: "))
12   mystery_number(num_in)
```

Q2) In the program above, four lines of code are redundant i.e. they can be removed without affecting the program's output, which four lines can be removed:

_____

Q3) Lines 6 and 7 state that when the number 3 is passed in, the

_____

_____

CHALLENGE 6: REFINING

Re-write the program from the previous page so that the program outputs 1 if the value of num is 3. It should output 8 if the number is less than 5 (but not 3). It should output the number entered for all other cases.

Hint: You will need to re-order the if statement.

CHALLENGE 7: PARSON'S PUZZLE

Parson's puzzles are named after Dale Parsons[1]. To solve the puzzle, re-arrange the code blocks into the correct order. The subprogram should take two numbers as arguments and subtract the smallest number from the largest. The result is returned.

A
```
num1_in = int(input("Enter a number"))
num2_in = int(input("Enter a number"))

difference = subtract(num1_in, num2_in)

print("The difference is", difference)
```

B
```
def subtract(num1, num2):
```

C
```
    return out
```

D
```
    else:
        out = num2 - num1
```

E
```
    if num1 > num2:
        out = num1 - num2
```

Correct order:

[1]Keen students may think that there is a misplaced apostrophe here. However, in Parsons' original paper co-authored with Patricia Haden in 2006, they are referred to as "Parson's puzzles". Some refer to them as "Parsons problems" or simply "Parsons".

CHALLENGE 8: MULTIPLE CHOICE QUESTIONS

Circle the correct answer to the questions below.

1) What is the difference between a function and a procedure:

A.   A function has parameters, a procedure does not

B.   A function returns a value, a procedure does not

C.   A procedure returns a value, a function does not

D.   A procedure has parameters, a function does not

2) The program below can be translated as:

```
if num1 > 9:
```

A.   If num1 is greater than or equal to 9

B.   If 9 is greater than num1

C.   If num1 is greater than 9

D.   If num1 is less than 9

3) Values passed into parameters are known as:

A.   Variables

B.   Functions

C.   Arguments

D.   Integers or Strings

4) What is the keyword used to define a function in Python:

A.   function

B.   define

C.   sub

D.   def

STRING CONCATENATION: MAKING A USERNAME

A subprogram which outputs a username based on a student's first name, surname and year of enrolment.

E.g. Connor Pearce 2019 should return 19CPearce.

```
1   def user_name(forename, last_name, year):
2      username_out = year[2:4] + forename[0] + last_name
3
4      print("Your user name is " + username_out)
5
6
7   first_name = input("Enter your first name: ")
8   surname = input("Enter your surname: ")
9   joined = input("Enter the year you joined the school: ")
10
11  user_name(first_name,surname,joined)
```

- The procedure `user_name` is defined on lines 1-4.
- Line 2: Strings can be sliced, with the first index being 0. In this case for the year, we start at 2 and stop at 4 (exclusive). This means we would slice year[2] and year[3] i.e. the last two digits of the `year`. These are concatenated with the first letter from the `forename` and the entire `last_name`.
- Lines 7-9: This shows how the procedure might be used. First the user's details are taken as string inputs .
- Then the procedure is called on line 11 with the user's details as arguments.
- The output is shown below:

```
Enter your first name: Connor
Enter your surname: Pearce
Enter the year you joined the school: 2019
Your username is 19CPearce
```

STRING CONCATENATION: MAKING A USERNAME CONTINUED...

If you wanted to use this `user_name` procedure later to generate an email address, this would not be possible without duplication of code, it is therefore wise to rewrite this subprogram as a function. This is shown below:

```
1   def user_name(forename, last_name, year):
2       username_out = year[2:4] + forename[0] + last_name
3
4       return username_out
5
6
7   def main():
8       first_name = input("Enter your first name: ")
9       surname = input("Enter your surname: ")
10      year = input("Enter the year you joined the school: ")
11
12      gen_user_name = user_name(first_name, surname, year)
13      print("Your user name is " + gen_user_name)
14
15
16  if __name__ == '__main__':
17      main()
```

Here we introduce a programming convention of placing your main program in a main function. The main function should be the only function which contains inputs and ouputs in the entire program. From this main function you should call other functions, passing arguments into parameters. This process is known as parameter passing.

The main function above spans lines 7-13. Lines 16-17 ensure that your main function will be the first function to be run when the program is executed. __name__ == '__main__' by default. However, if the program is imported, the __name__ value becomes the module name, so you can selectively run or test functions. This is yet another advantage of using the functional programming paradigm.

18

CHALLENGE 9: INITIALS ONLY

Write a subprogram that takes three strings as arguments: a first name, a middle name and a last name. The program should take these three arguments and return only the first letter of each string thereby generating initials.

```
def initials_only(first, middle, last):

    initials =


    return
```

CHALLENGE 10: SUBJECT SHORTENER

On school timetables, subjects are often shortened to their first 3 characters e.g. Maths becomes Mat, French becomes Fre and Music becomes Mus.

Write a subprogram that has a parameter called subject, this takes the subject as an argument and the program will return the shortened subject name.

CALCULATE THE AREA OF A CIRCLE

A subprogram which calculates the area of a circle.

The example below is a function as it returns a value.

```
1   CONSTANT_PI=3.14159
2
3   def circle_area(radius_in):
4       area_out = CONSTANT_PI * radius_in**2
5       return area_out
6
7
8   radius = int(input("Enter the radius of the circle: "))
9   area = circle_area(radius)
10  print("The area of the circle is", area)
```

- Line 1: As the value of Pi *will not change whilst the program is running*, this is a constant. Programmers sometimes write constants in capitals and may give them meaningful names as shown.
- Line 3: The function `circle_area` is defined and has one parameter (a placeholder/variable) called `radius_in`.
- The `area_out` is calculated radius**2 may also be written as radius ^2 in other languages and psuedocode.
- Lines 8-10: This shows how the function may be used.
- Line 9: The `circle_area` is called and the `radius` is passed as an argument. The result is stored in the variable `area`.
- Line 10: In Python, we can also use a comma to concatenate the `area` to the output message. The advantage of using a comma to concatenate is that casting is done implicitly. This means the `str()` function is not necessary. It is worth noting that concatenating with a comma will automatically add a space between concatenated strings.

CHALLENGE 11: VOLUME OF A CUBOID

Write a subprogram that takes the length, width and height as arguments and return the volume of the cuboid.

After writing the function, show how you might call the function to output an answer with a meaningful message.

CHALLENGE 12: ADD

Write a subprogram called `add` which has two parameters, `num1` and `num2`. The two numbers that are passed in should be added to each other and returned to the user.

```python
def add (num1,num2):
    sum = num1 + num2
    return sum


num1_in = int(input("Enter a number"))
num2_in = int(input("Enter another \
number"))


total = add(num1_in,num2_in)


print("The sum of the two numbers is \
" + str(total))
```

CHALLENGE 13: MULTIPLE CHOICE QUESTIONS

Circle the correct answer to the questions below.

1) What is the output of the following:
```
name = "Shenaz"
print(name[3:5])
```
A. 345
B. en
C. na
D. naz

2) What is the output of the following:
```
subject = "Computer Science"
print(subject[1])
```
A. C
B. o
C. 1
D. Co

3) What is the result of 2**3 ?:
A. 6
B. 23
C. 2**3
D. 8

4) What is a constant ?:
A. A variable which stays the same whilst the program is running
B. A value which can not change whilst the program is running
C. A numerical value
D. Part of a formula which is defined

ODD OR EVEN?

A subprogram which checks if a number is odd or even. It will print a meaningful message accordingly. The program should loop until the user enters the sentinel value "STOP"

This is a procedure as no value is returned.

```
1   def is_odd(number_in):
2       if int(number_in) %2 == 0:
3           print("The number is even")
4       else:
5           print("The number is odd")
6
7
8   again = True
9   while again:
10    number = input("Enter a number")
11
12    if number != "STOP" :
13        odd = is_odd(number)
14    else:
15        again = False
```

- Line 2: The % symbol in Python means MODULO. So when we MOD2, we are checking for the remainder when dividing by 2
- Line 8: Sets a Boolean flag called `again` to True.
- Line 9: This is a Pythonic way of writing `while again == True:`
- Lines 11-12: Provided the user does not enter the sentinel value (also known as a rogue or trip value) of "STOP", the while loop will continue to call `is_odd` with each new number inputted to check if it is odd or even.

CHALLENGE 14: ODD OR EVEN FUNCTION

The Odd or Even program could be improved by using a function instead of a procedure. Re-write the program so that all inputs and outputs take place outside of the is_odd function. You could also use a main function as shown previously on page 23.

CHALLENGE 15: IS X A MULTIPLE OF Y

Given that we can use MODULO to see if there is a remainder, we can write a subprogram which tells us if a given number x is a multiple of y.

E.g. if x is 18 and y is 9, the subprogram should output a meaningful message to tell us that 18 is a multiple of 9. If x is 20 and y is 7, the subprogram should output a meaningful message to tell us 20 is not a multiple of 7.

```
_____ is_multiple (x_in,        ):
   if                              == 0:
      print(                                    )
   else:
      print(x_in, "is not a multiple of", y_in)


print("A program to check if x is a multiple of y")
x = int(input("Enter a number to check if it is a multiple"))
y = int(input("Enter a number to divide by"))
#Call the procedure, passing in x and y

_____

```

CHALLENGE 16: TRACING WITH DIV

While % (MODULO) returns the remainder from a division. We can also do Integer division, also known as floor division or DIV by using // . Using // ignores any remainder and always rounds down.

e.g. 10 DIV 5 = 2   (10 goes in 5 two times)

      10 DIV 3 = 3   (10 goes into 3 three times, we ignore the 1 remainder)

      4 DIV 3 = 0   (4 does not go into 3, we ignore the 4 remainder)

      3 DIV 4 = 1   (3 goes into 4 once, we ignore the 1 remainder)

1) State the output for the following program when the program is run four times with four different inputs:

num1	num2	Output
1	8	
3	9	
14	10	
21		4

```
1   def div(num1_in, num2_in):
2       out = (num1+num2) // 10
3           return out
4
5   num1 = int(input("Enter your first number"))
6   num2 = int(input("Enter your second number"))
7
8   floor = div(num1,num2)
9   print(floor)
10
```

2) Calculate the following:

a) 21 DIV 7 = _____

b) 9 DIV 4 = _____

c) 8 DIV 3 = _____

FOR LOOPS: OUTPUTTING NUMBERS

A subprogram which outputs all the numbers between a certain start and stop value (inclusive).

Here we will use a for loop (also known as a count-controlled loop) as we know exactly how many times we want to loop based on the start and stop values. It is a definite loop.

This is a procedure as it does not return a value.

```
1   def number_generator(start, stop):
2       for count in range(start,stop+1):
3           print(count)
4
5
6   start_num = int(input("Enter a start value"))
7   stop_num = int(input("Enter a stop value"))
8
9   number_generator(start_num, stop_num)
```

- The procedure number_generator is defined on lines 1-3.
- Line 2: uses a for loop to iterate from the start value to the stop value. In Python, the stop value is exclusive, so number_generator(1,10) would only print numbers 1 to 9, this is why we use stop+1.
- Lines 6-9 show how we would use the procedure.
- Lines 6-7: The user's details are taken as inputs .
- Then the procedure is called on line 9.

WHILE LOOPS: NUMBER GUESSER

A program which generates a random number then asks the user to guess the random number. The program repeats until the correct number is guessed.

As we do not know how many guesses the user will need to guess the number correctly, we use a while loop (also known as a condition-controlled loop). It is an indefinite loop.

This is a function as the smallest number is returned.

```
1   import random
2   randomNumber = random.randint(1,10)
3   guess = 99
4   while guess != randomNumber:
5       guess = int(input("Guess the number between 1 and \
    10: "))
6       if guess == randomNumber:
7           print("Correct")
8       else:
9           print("Try again")
```

- Line 1: Imports the `random` module so that we can use the `randint` function to generate a random integer between 1 and 10 (inclusive).
- Unlike the previous program, we do not know how many times we need to repeat; the user could get the answer wrong 8 times or they could guess it first time. In these situations we use a conditional loop i.e. a while loop.
- Line 3: Sets an initial value that will never match the random number. This ensures the while loop runs at least once.
- Lines 8-9: If the user guess is incorrect, we return to the top of the loop i.e. line 5.

UNLIMITED PIN ATTEMPTS

A program which allows the user to enter a pin number. If the user gets the pin number wrong, the program keeps asking them to enter a correct pin.

N.B. An unlimited number of attempts is a bad idea as it allows for brute force hacking. However, this is a common algorithm that is used in guessing games e.g. guess the number.

```
1  pin = ""
2  while pin != "1984":
3      pin = input("Please enter the pin")
4
5      if pin == "1984":
6          print("Logged in")
7      else:
8          print("Incorrect pin")
```

- The program keeps looping while the pin is not equal to 1984. It is very similar to the program on page 11.
- Line 1: Sets an initial value that is not equal to the pin. This ensures the while loop runs at least once.
- Line 3 asks the user to enter their pin.
- Lines 5-8 check to see if the pin matches, a meaningful message is produced depending on the outcome.

BASIC LOGIN SYSTEM

A program which checks to see if the username and password matches the one in our program. The user gets three attempts.

```
1    username = "James"
2    password = "myPasswordIsDog!"
3    pass_in = ""
4    tries = 0
5
6    while tries < 3 and pass_in != password:
7        user_in = input("Enter the username: ")
8        pass_in = input("Enter the password: ")
9
10       if user_in == username:
11           if pass_in == password:
12               print("Logged in")
13           else:
14               print("Incorrect password")
15       else:
16           print("Incorrect username")
17
18       tries = tries+1
```

- Line 3: Initialises the `pass_in` variable with an empty string so that the while loop on Line 6 runs at least once
- Line 4: Initialises a while loop counter called `tries` to 0.
- Line 5: The while loop provides a maximum of 3 password attempts. We use a while loop because we do not know how many attempts the user will need to get the answer correct.
- Lines 10-12: If the correct `username` and `password` is supplied, we output a "logged in" message. Otherwise, a meaningful error message is shown and the `tries` variable is incremented (Line 18).
- Line 18: This is also a common way to increase a score or counter.
- N.B. Storing the password as plaintext in the program that you are using is a really bad idea! Curious readers should visit: http://bit.do/hashing-python-passwords for more info.

CHALLENGE 17: ACRONYM GENERATOR

Recall challenge 9 on page 24. The program works well for people with a first name, middle name and last name. However, some people do not have middle names and some people have more than one. In other scenarios, you may wish to simply generate some acronyms to shorten several words e.g.
Graphic Interchange Format can be shortened to GIF and British Broadcasting Corporation can be shortened to BBC.

The program below should ask the user for a word and keep asking for words until the characters "XXX" are entered. "XXX" acts as a sentinel value or rogue value which stops a loop from running. When the sentinel value is entered, the program should stop asking for words and an acronym should be generated and output

```
sentinel = "XXX"  #The sentinel value

word = ""

acronym = ""

while word !=                     :

   word = input("Enter a word or "XXX" to
finish")

   if word != sentinel:

      acronym = acronym + word[      ]


print(                         )
```

CHALLENGE 18: ACRONYM GENERATOR 2.0

The previous acronym generator program is inefficient as the user has to enter each word separately and has to enter a sentinel value.

Fill in the gaps in the program below to make a more efficient program which takes several words and generates an acronym based on the first character of each word.

N.B. in the program below we can iterate through each word in the words string by using the line `for word in words:`
This means the same as
`for count in range (len(words)):`

```
acronym = ""
words = input("Enter words to be turned
into an acronym")
#Convert words into a list of indivudal words
words_list = words.split()
#For each word in the words_list
for word in words_list:
    acronym =                  + words_list[    ]

print
```

CHALLENGE 19: ROLL A DOUBLE TO START

Write a program which simulates two dice being rolled. Output the values of both dice. Keep prompting the user to roll the dice until the two dice match e.g. Double 6. When the user roles a double, output the message "Game loading". For all other combinations, ask the user to press Enter to roll again.

Remember, when we do not know how many times we need to run the loop, this is a conditional loop i.e. a while loop.

CHALLENGE 20: KEEPING SCORE OVER THREE ROUNDS

Write a program which simulates two dice being rolled three times. Output the total value of both dice for each roll. Keep track of the score over 3 rounds and output the total at the end

Hint: As we know that the pair of dice are rolled three times, this repetition is fixed. We therefore need to use a count-controlled loop i.e. a for loop.

LOWEST NUMBER IN A LIST

A program which iterates through a list of numbers and outputs the lowest number

```
1  numbers_list = [9,8,7,5,6,2,1,12,14,0,13]
2
3  lowest = numbers_list[0]
4
5  for count in range(len(numbers_list)):
6       if numbers_list[count] < lowest:
7            lowest = numbers_list[count]
8
9  print("The lowest number in the list is ", lowest)
```

- Line 3: We start with the hypothesis that the item at position 0 of `numbers_list` is the lowest.
- Line 5: We then iterate through the full length of the list, comparing each position with the initial value stored in `lowest`.
- Lines 6-7 If the current value is smaller than `lowest`, this number replaces the item in `lowest`.
- Line 9: When the for loop has finished and we have therefore reached the end of the list, we output the value of `lowest`.
- This can also be written as a function which takes a list as an argument.

```
1  def find_lowest(numbers_list_in):
2     lowest = numbers_list_in[0]
3
4     for count in range(len(numbers_list_in)):
5        if numbers_list_in[count] < lowest:
6           lowest = numbers_list_in[count]
7
8     return lowest
9
10 numbers_list = [9,8,7,5,6,2,1,12,14,0,13]
11 lowest_num = find_lowest(numbers_list)
12 print("The lowest number in the list is ", lowest_num)
```

LINEAR SEARCH

Iterating through a list from start to finish as seen in the previous algorithm is effectively a linear search. We start at position 0 and continue checking each position from left to right until we reach the end. A meaningful message informs the user whether the item was found.

```
1   def linear_search(target):
2       names = ["Elizabeth", "Samuel", "Jawwad",
3               "Yacoub", "Cara", "Jess",
4               "Benji", "Thamber", "Suki", "Zi", "Q"]
5
6       found = False
7
8       for count in range(len(names)):
9           if target == (names[count]):
10              print(target, "found at position", count)
11              found = True
12
13      if found == False:
14          print(target, "was not found")
15
16
17  name = input("Who are you looking for? ")
18  linear_search(name)
```

- For all searching algorithms, you should start by setting a Boolean flag to False. We do this on line 6.
- Lines 9-11: If the target matches the item in the array, the name is outputted and the Boolean flag is set to True.
- Lines 13-14: When we've iterated through the entire list, check to see if found is still False. If so, the item was not in the list.
- Line 18: Notice how we pass the argument stored in the variable called name into the parameter called target. The argument and parameter name are different so that we understand that their scope is different. The footnote on page 5 explains this in more detail.

CHALLENGE 21: HIGHEST NUMBER IN A LIST

Write a program which iterates through a list of numbers and outputs the highest number

```
numbers = [9, 8, 72, 22, 21, 81, 2, 1,]
```

CHALLENGE 22: HIGHEST NUMBER IN A LIST FUNCTION

Re-write the program from the previous page as a subprogram. The list of numbers should be passed in as an argument. The subprogram should then iterate through a list of numbers and return the highest number

```
numbers = [9, 8, 72, 22, 21, 81, 2, 1]
```

CHALLENGE 23: WEAK PASSWORD?

Write a program which asks the user to enter a desired password. Perform a linear search through a list of obvious weak passwords. If the user's password is found in the obvious passwords list, output a message to tell them it is weak and would be easily hacked using a brute force attack.

```
obvious = ["password", "qwerty",
"hello123", "letmein", "123456"]
```

CHALLENGE 24: WEAK PASSWORD CONTINUED

Add in various validation checks to the program on the previous page. One example might be a length check, so if the password does not meet a particular length it is also declared weak. Other checks could be a presence check and format check. The format check could check to see if the user entered any numbers, symbols and a mixture of upper and lower case letters. Meaningful messages are necessary for each different validation check.

CHALLENGE 25: PENALTY SHOOTOUT

Write a program which simulates a penalty shootout. The computer is the goalkeeper and dives a random direction or stays in the centre each turn. The keeper's move is generated but not outputted at first. The user takes a penalty by typing in "left", "right" or "centre". The keeper's move is then outputted. If the player typed left and the keeper dives left, the penalty is saved etc. The program repeats 5 times. After 5 penalties, the winner is announced with a meaningful message.

Hint: Pages 29 and 30. I strongly advise using a pencil for this one!

```python
import random


keeper = ["left", "centre", "right"]
```

```python
# More space on next page...
```

CHALLENGE 25: PENALTY SHOOTOUT CONTINUED...

More space on next page...

CHALLENGE 25: PENALTY SHOOTOUT CONTINUED...

CHALLENGE 26: TRACING LOOPS

1) Write the values of x and y for the program below:

x	y
0	
1	

```
1    y = 0
2
3    for x in range(0,4):
4        if x % 2 == 0:
5            y = x + 2
6            print(y)
```

2) Re-write the for loop (line 3) below if we wanted the x value to loop from 1 to 10:

_____

3) What is the purpose of line 1 of the program above?

_____

_____

_____

_____

CHALLENGE 27: MULTIPLE CHOICE QUESTIONS

Circle the correct answer based on the following code:

```
import random
for count in range(0,5):
  num1=random.randint(1,10)
```

1) What are the highest and lowest possible values of num1?
A.   10 and 1
B.   10 and 0
C.   9 and 1
D.   9 and 0

2) What are the first and last values of count if they were outputted?
A.   0 and 5
B.   0 and 4
C.   1 and 5
D.   1 and 4

3) How many times does the for loop repeat?
A.   5 times
B.   0 times
C.   4 times
D.   6 times

4) Given a list called sentence which consists of 5 words, other than `for count in range(5),` how else can you iterate through each word in the sentence?

TOTAL OF A LIST

A program which adds up numbers in a list

```
1   number_list = [9, 8, 3, 5, 4, 1, 8, 4, 1]
2
3   total = 0
4
5   for count in range(len(number_list)):
6       total = total + number_list[count]
7
8   print("The total sum of the list is ", total)
```

- Line 3: Defines the variable `total` and initialises it to 0.
- Line 5: Iterates through the length of the list, 0 to 9 (exclusive).
- Line 6: Takes the current value of total and adds the current value in the list to the total. This cumulative total is commonly used for scores and timers in programs.
- A functional programming approach is also shown below:

```
1   def total_list (number_list_in):
2       total = 0
3
4       for count in range(len(number_list)):
5           total = total + number_list[count]
6
7       return total #the total is returned
8
9
10  def main():
11      # The main function contains all inputs and outputs
12      number_list = [9, 8, 3, 5, 4, 1, 8, 4, 1]
13
14      op = input("Do you wish to find the mean, lowest \
    value, highest value or the total of the list?")
15
16      # Call the relevant function based on the user input
17      if op == "total":
18          total_out = total_list(number_list)
19          print("The total sum of the list is ", total_out)
20      # Elifs would go here
21
22  # Call the main function
23  main()
```

CHALLENGE 28: AVERAGE OF A LIST

Write a subprogram called mean_of_list that takes a list of numbers as an argument and returns the mean average.

Write the main function which contains your list and which calls the subprogram (function)

CHALLENGE 29: COUNTING VOWELS

Iterate through the sentence below and count how many times each vowel occurs. At the end of the program, ouput the number of As, Es, Is, Os and Us with a meaningful message.

sentence = "Learning programming is similar to learning a musical instrument. Both involve practise and making lots of mistakes. Both also require perseverance to develop fluency. Keep going!"

```
def vowel_counter(sentence):

    A = 0

    E = 0

    I = 0



    for _____

        if sentence[          ].upper() == "A":
```

More space on next page...

LINEAR SEARCH IN A 2D LIST

A program which searches for a student's results within a 2D list of exam scores.[1]

```
1   cs_scores=[["Jo","45","60","72"],["Zi","55","65","70"],
2   ["Ellie","71","78","78"],["Jessica","68","79","80"],
3   ["Taseen","65","70","71"]]
4
5   print("We will try to find the result for a given \
    student's exam")
6
7   name = input("Enter a student name: ")
8   exam_number = int(input("Enter the exam number: "))
9
10  found = False
11
12  for count in range(len(cs_scores)):
13      if name == cs_scores[count][0]:
14          found = True
15          result = cs_scores[count][exam_number]
16          print(name+ "'s result for exam", exam_number,\
    "was", result )
17
18  if found == False:
19      print(name, "cannot be found")
```

- Line 10: Use a variable to set a Boolean flag to False.
- Lines 12-14: if the name is located, the `found` flag is set to True and the result can be found by indexing the 2D list using the current `count` and the `exam_number`.
- Line 18: if we reach the end of the list and found is still False, then the number was not in the list.
- Lines 16 and 19: Output a meaningful message.

[1]Python does not have an array data structure. Instead it uses a list. The main differences between a list and an array is that lists allow the storage of mixed data types and they are dynamic (allow appending). I've tried to use single data types with the lists in this book so they appear more like arrays. I have also avoided the use of in-built list functions. This may seem strange and inefficient in places but it has been done as the GCSE exam will only feature arrays.

CHALLENGE 30: GRADE BOUNDARIES

An A-Level student wants to find out how many marks are required to receive a certain grade. Write a subprogram that takes a user's desired grade as an argument and then iterates through the 2D list to return the number of marks they need for that grade.

```
def _____ ( _____ ) :
    grades = [ ["A*", "90"], ["A", "83",],
    ["B", "72"], ["C", "60"], ["D", "49"],
    ["E", "30"] ]
```

CHALLENGE 31: COUNTING VOWELS 2D LIST

Use a 2D List to improve challenge 29; keeping track of how many times each vowel occurs in the sentence below. At the end of the program, ouput the number of As, Es, Is, Os and Us with a meaningful message.

sentence = "Learning programming is similar to learning a musical instrument. Both involve practise and making lots of mistakes. Both also require perseverance to develop fluency. Keep going!"

TOTAL OF A 2D LIST

A program which adds up each student's scores in a 2D list i.e. a row or sub list

```
1   cs_scores = [["Karman","45","60","72"],
2                ["Daniel","55","65","70"],
3                ["Parker","71","78","78"],
4                ["Jessica","68","79","80"],
5                ["Edie","98","85","91"]]
6
7   total = 0
8   for student in range(len(cs_scores)):
9       for exam in range(1,4):
10          total = total + int(cs_scores[student][exam])
11      print("Total for",cs_scores[student][0],"=",total)
12      total = 0
```

- In the program above we are trying to calculate each student's total, so the student is in the first loop. This is also known as the outer loop.
- Line 8: Iterate through 0 to 5 (exclusive) i.e. each student .
- Line 9: Now starting with student 0 i.e. Karman, enter the nested inner loop through exams 1 to 4 (exclusive) i.e. exams 1-3.
- Line 10: Add the score to the running total.
- Line 11: Output the student's total.
- Line 12: Reset the `total` variable to 0 so that we can now start the second iteration of the student loop and calculate the total of Daniel's exams.

CHALLENGE 32: TOTAL FOR EACH EXAM IN A 2D LIST

Write a program which will output the total for each exam with a meaningful message.

Hint: As the focus is on each *exam* rather than each student, the outer for loop will be for each *exam*. Remember to reset the total after each iteration of the inner loop.

```
cs_scores = [["Karman","45","60","72"],
["Daniel","55","65","70"],
["Parker","71","78","78"],
["Jessica","68","79","80"],
["Edie","98","85","91"]]


total = 0


for exam in range(                    ):
```

CHALLENGE 33: AVERAGE FOR EACH STUDENT IN A 2D LIST

Write a program that outputs the mean average for each student.

Hint: Remember to reset the total to 0 after outputting the average for each student

```
cs_scores = [["Theo","45","60","72"],
["Angharad","55","65","70"],
["Sameer","71","78","78"],
["Adrian","68","79","80"],
["Ayana","98","85","91"]]
```

CHALLENGE 34: AVERAGE FOR EACH STUDENT IN A 2D LIST

Re-write challenge 33 so that it is a subprogram. The subprogram should take the 2D list of exam results as an argument and output the mean average for each student.

```
cs_scores = [["Theo","45","60","72"],
["Angharad","55","65","70"],
["Sameer","71","78","78"],
["Adrian","68","79","80"],
["Ayana","98","85","91"]]
```

CHALLENGE 35: TRACING LOOPS

1) Write the values of x and y for the first 5 iterations of the program below:

x	y	output
0		

```
1    animals = [["Charlie", "Dog", 8],
2                ["Dolly", "Sheep", 3],
3                ["Wanda", "Goldfish", 4]]
4
5    for x in range(len(animals)):
6       for y in range(0,3):
7          print(animals[x][y])
```

2) What is the name of the data structure on lines 1-3?

_____

3) The Nested for loop on line 5-7 is an example of which programming construct?

A.   Sequence

B.   Selection

C.   Iteration

CHALLENGE 36: MULTIPLE CHOICE QUESTIONS

Circle the correct answer based on the following code:

```
for x in range(0,3):
    for y in range(2,5):
        z = x + y
        print(z)
```

1) What is output when the program above is run?
A.   0,1,2,2,3,4
B.   2,3,4,5,3,4,5,6,3,4,5,6
C.   0,1,2,3,2,3,4,5
D.   2,3,4,5,6,3,4,5,6,7,4,5,6,7,8,5,6,7,8,

2) Given the code in Challenge 35 and given that
`print(animals[1][2])` gives the output of 3. What does
`print(animals[2][0])` output?
A.   3, 0
B.   4
C.   Wanda
D.   Dolly

3) Referring again to challenge 35, what would be output if the
following code was run `print(animals[3][3])`
A.   3, 3
B.   Logic error
C.   Syntax error
D.   Index error: list index out of range

LOGIN SYSTEM BY READING A 2D LIST IN A FILE

A procedure which performs a linear search on a 2D list that is stored in a file.

users.txt
[['lauw', 'insecurePwd'], ['vegaj', 'iLoveWebDesign'], ['lassamil', 'zeroDawn']]

```
1   def login():
2       username = input("What is your username")
3       password = input("What is your password")
4
5       newfile = open("users.txt","r")
6       users_2D = eval(newfile.read())
7       newfile.close()
8
9       found = False
10      for count in range(len(users_2D)):
11          if username == users_2D[count][0]:
12              found = True
13              if password == users_2D[count][1]:
14                  print("logged in")
15              else:
16                  print("incorrect password")
17                  login()
18
19      if found==False:
20          print("Invalid username")
21          login()
22
23  login()
```

- Line 5: Opens the file `users.txt` in read mode.
- Line 6: Reads the file. We have used the `eval` function which means that the translator will treat the text file's contents as a Python expression if the format is valid. In this case, it converts the contents of the text file into a 2D list and stores this under the identifier `users_2D`.
- Lines 17 and 21: calls the `login` procedure if the login fails i.e. it restarts the procedure.

CHALLENGE 37: UNIQUE USERNAME

Write a subprogram which generates a username for a teacher based on their first name and surname. The format should be their surname, followed by the first letter of their first name. The program should check to see if the username already exists in users.txt and if so, a unique username should be generated by appending a "#" symbol. E.g. if a teacher joins the school called Winnie Lau, their username would be LauW# . The username should then be returned.

users.txt
[['LauW', 'insecurePwd'], ['VegaJ', 'iLoveWebDesign'], ['LassamiL', 'zeroDawn']]

```python
def generate_username(firstname, lastname):

    username =


    #check to see if the username already exists

    users_file = open(                    ,        )

    usernames = eval(                    )

    users_file.close()


    for count in range(len(                )):

        if                        == username:

            username =

    return
```

CHALLENGE 38: USING THE UNIQUE USERNAME SUBPROGRAM

Write a program which asks for a teacher's first name and surname. Then demonstrate how you would call the function on the previous page to generate a username and output this in a meaningful message.

_____

_____

_____

_____

_____

_____

_____

_____

_____

_____

_____

The next pages is provided so that you can practise Challenge 37 again without the writing frame. It's important that you keep challenging yourself and eventually you should be able to write these programs independently.

CHALLENGE 37: UNIQUE USERNAME

Write a subprogram which generates a username for a teacher based on their first name and surname. The format should be their surname, followed by the first letter of their first name. The program should check to see if the username already exists in users.txt and if so, a unique username should be generated by appending a "#" symbol. E.g. if a teacher joins the school called Winnie Lau, their username would be LauW# . The username should then be returned.

users.txt
[['LauW', 'insecurePwd'], ['VegaJ', 'iLoveWebDesign'], ['LassamiL', 'zeroDawn']]

WRITING A SHOPPING LIST TO A FILE

File writing is essential if you want to save data permanently to your programs. This allows you to open a program and read in data. Examples of data might be a shopping list, usernames and passwords, player names and scores. The program below asks a user for shopping list items to be written to a file.

Type this out to check if a shopping_list.txt file is created next to your Python file and to check if your shopping list is written there.

```
1   def shopping():
2       item = ' '
3       items = []
4       while item != 'End':
5           item = input('Enter a shopping list item or \
6   enter "End" to finish your list.').title()
7
8           if item != 'End':
9               items.append(item)
10
11      newfile = open("shopping_list.txt","w")
12      newfile.write(str(items))
13      newfile.close()
14
15  shopping()
```

- Line 2: Sets a default or initial value for item . This allows the while loop on line 4 to run at least once
- Line 3: Creates an empty list which will append to on line 8
- Lines 5-6: Allows the user to keep entering items and casts their item to title case i.e. capital letter on the first character.
- Lines 7-8: Checks if the item is "End" and if not, it appends the item to the items list.
- Line 9: Opens a file in write mode. If one does not exist, it will create a new file. If it already exists, it will overwrite the content.
- Line 10: Writes the list as a string into newfile.

N.B. You can only write strings to files, so lists have to be cast.

ADDING TO A LIST IN A FILE

On the previous page, we learnt that opening a file in write mode will erase the previous data if the file already exists. There are two ways of adding to an existing file. However, when we are dealing with lists in Python, the best approach is to read in a list from the file, append to the list and then overwrite the file with this updated list. This is shown below.

Shopping_list.txt
['Rice', 'Ackee', 'Peppers', 'Tomatoes']

```
1    def add_shopping():
2        item = ' '
3        file = open("shopping_list.txt","r")
4        items = eval(file.read())
5        file.close()
6
7        while item != 'End':
8            item = input('Enter a shopping list item or \
9    enter "End" to finish your list.').title()
10
11           if item != 'End':
12               items.append(item)
13
14       newfile = open("shopping_list.txt","w")
15       newfile.write(str(items))
16       newfile.close()
17
18   add_shopping()
```

We have only changed lines 3-5, these open the file in read mode and evaluates the contents into a list called items.

If you have paired sets of data e.g. player names and scores or usernames and passwords, you may want to use a 2D list in a file. The rest of the code stays the same. However, it's worth noting that storing the password as plaintext may be fine for GCSE Computer Science, but in real applications, it is a really bad idea! Curious readers should visit: http://bit.do/hashing-python-passwords for more info.

CHALLENGE 39: REGISTER AN ACCOUNT

Write a subprogram to allow a teacher to register a new account. The subprogram should take the username and password as arguments and write these details to the existing users.txt file shown opposite.

Hint: Use the comments on the opposite page as skeleton code to structure your subprogram

```
def new_user(username_in, password_in):


    users =



    new_user = []
    new_user.append(username_in)



    users.append(new_user)
    users_file = open(                      , "w")
                        .write(str(          )
```

CHALLENGE 39: REGISTER AN ACCOUNT CONTINUED...

users.txt
[['lauw', 'insecurePwd'], ['vegaj', 'iLoveWebDesign'], ['lassamil', 'zeroDawn']]

```
# define a function new_user with two parameters:
# username and password


# open the file in read mode


# use eval to read in the 2D list


# close the file




# make a new list for the new user


# append the username to the new user list


# append the password to the same list




# append this new user list to the existing 2D list that
# we read in

# open the file in write mode


# cast the updated 2D list as a string and write this
string to the file

# close the file

```

72

CHALLENGE 40: MULTIPLE CHOICE QUESTIONS

1) To append to the end of a file we should use?

A.   file.append("some text")

B.   file = open("txtfile.txt", "a")
       file.write("some text")

C.   file = open("txtfile.txt", "append")
       file.append("some text")

D.   file = "some text".append()

2) Opening a file in "w" mode will usually...:

A.   Allow you to write to a file, wiping the original data
B.   Allow you to write to the end of a file
C.   Allow you to write to the beginning of a file, keeping what is there
D.   Allow you to read or write from the file

3) After file operations, we should always

A.   Close the file
B.   Save the file with a new file name
C.   Loop back to the beginning of the file
D.   Open the file

CHALLENGE 41: PARSON'S PUZZLE

Solve the puzzle by re-arranging the code blocks into the correct order. The program should ask for a user's e-mail address and if it is in the 2D list stored in the file, it returns True otherwise it returns False.

A
```
file = open ("users.txt","r")

users = eval(file.read())
```

B
```
email = input("Enter a username")
```

C
```
file.close()
```

D
```
for count in range(len(users)):
```

E
```
return Found
```

F
```
    if email == users[count][0]:
        found = True
        return Found
```

G
```
found = False
```

Correct order:

CONVERTING BINARY TO DENARY

A subprogram which takes a 4-bit binary string as an argument and returns the denary equivalent

```
1   def binary_to_denary(binary):
2       bit1 = int(binary[3])*1
3       bit2 = int(binary[2])*2
4       bit3 = int(binary[1])*4
5       bit4 = int(binary[0])*8
6
7       denary_out = bit1 + bit2 + bit3 + bit4
8       return denary_out
9
10
11  def main():
12      binary_in = input("Enter the binary string")
13      denary = binary_to_denary(binary_in)
14      print("The binary value", binary_in, "in denary \
        is", denary)
15
16
17  if __name__ == '__main__':
18      main()
```

- Lines 17-18: The default value for __name__ in every Python program is '__main__' and so the main function is called.
- Line 12: Asks the user for a binary string.
- Line 13: Calls the binary_to_denary function, passing the binary string as an argument. The returned value will be stored in the denary variable and output on Line 14.
- Line 1: Defines a function called binary_to_denary and takes the binary_in string as an argument.
- Lines 2-5: Slices each individual digit and multiplies it by its relevant place value.
- Lines 7-8: The total is calculated and returned.
- Line 14: The denary equivalent is outputted with a meaningful message.

CONVERTING DENARY TO BINARY

A program which converts a denary value between 0-15 to a 4-bit binary value

```
1  denary = int(input("Enter the denary number between \
   0 and 15"))
2
3  binary = ["0","0","0","0"]
4
5  if denary > 15:
6     print("error")
7  if denary >=8 and denary <=15:
8     binary[0] = "1"
9     denary = denary - 8
10 if denary >=4:
11    binary[1] = "1"
12    denary = denary - 4
13 if denary >=2:
14    binary[2] = "1"
15    denary = denary - 2
16 if denary >=1:
17    binary[3] = "1"
18
19 for count in range(len(binary)):
20    print(binary[count],end="")
```

- Line 3: With binary numbers, we cannot use the integer data type. A default string of "0000" also cannot be used as strings in Python are not mutable. Having four bits like the previous program could work, but I would have to define and initialise each bit. This could create up to four lines of extra code. I therefore decided to use a list as lists are mutable.
- Lines 7-17: This models the "left-to-right" process of checking how many 8s, 4s, 2s and 1s go into a number between 0-15.
- Lines 19-20: This is a way to iterate through the list and print each element without commas, brackets and new lines. The end="" means at the end of each print, do not add anything, as a default end="\n" i.e. a new line at the end of every print.

CHALLENGE 42: CONVERTING HEXADECIMAL TO DENARY

Write a function which takes in 1 hexadecimal digit as an argument and returns the denary equivalent.

Write a main function which asks the user to input a hexadecimal value and then passes this value to the function you have written.

CHALLENGE 43: A COMPUTER SCIENCE QUIZ

Q1) What is the correct answer in Q1 below? Fill in the gap on the if statement on line 24

```
1  def correct(score_in):
2    print("Well Done, this is the correct answer")
3    score_in = score_in + 1
4    return score_in
5
6  def quiz():
7    score = 0
8
9    print("""
10   Why do computers need primary storage?
11
12   A) To provide fast access memory to the CPU in the \
13 form of RAM and ROM
14   B) To provide long term storage of files on a hard \
15 disk drive
16   C) To act as RAM and allow programs to keep running \
17 when RAM is full
18   D) To provide storage in case secondary storage runs\
19 out
20      """)
21
22   Q1 = input("Choose a letter").upper()
23
24   if Q1 == "_____":
25       score = correct(score)
26       print(score)
27
```

Q2) When the program is run, nothing happens. Explain why?

_____

_____

Q3) What is the purpose of line 7?

_____

_____

CHALLENGE 44: BINARY SEARCH

Examine the binary search program below.

N.B. Line 33 contains an integer placeholder %d, it is replaced with the contents of the `result` variable using % as a placeholder

```
1    # Binary search returns location of target in given
2    # list if present, else returns -1
3    def binarySearch(nums, target):
4        left = 0
5        right = len(nums)-1
6        while left <= right:
7
8            mid = left + (right - left) // 2
9
10           # Check if target is present at mid
11           if nums[mid] == target:
12               return mid
13
14           # If x is greater, ignore left half
15           elif nums[mid] < target:
16               left = mid + 1
17
18           # If x is smaller, ignore right half
19           else:
20               right = mid - 1
21
22       # If we reach here, then the element was
23       # not present
24       return -1
25
26   nums_in = [ 2, 3, 4, 10, 40 ]
27   target_in = int(input("Enter a number to see if it \
28   is in the list"))
29
30   result = binarySearch(nums_in, target_in)
31
32   if result != -1:
33       print ("Element is present at index %d" %result)
34   else:
35       print ("Element is not present in array")
36
```

CHALLENGE 44: BINARY SEARCH CONTINUED...

Q1) What line is the function called on?

Q2) What is the name of the data structure on line 26?

Q3) How many parameters does the binarySearch function have?

Q4) When the program is run and the target_in is 10, what is the output?

Q5) When the program is run and the target_in is 20, what are the mid values that are examined?

Q6) The // on line 8 is a DIV operator. Explain what is meant by DIV

Q7) What is the data type of target_in on line 27?

CHALLENGE 45: STORE DISCOUNT

Examine the program below which is used to issue store discount

N.B. Line 24 contains a float placeholder %.2f, it is replaced with the contents of the total variable formatted to 2 decimal places using % as a placeholder

```
1    discounts = [["summer10",0.1],
2                 ["welcome",0.15],
3                 ["refer20",0.2]]
4
5    discount = 0
6
7    total = float(input("What is the order total: £"))
8    discount_in = input("Do you have a discount \
9    code?").lower()
10
11   if discount_in == "yes":
12     discountcode = input("Enter a discount code").lower()
13
14     valid = False
15
16
17
18
19
20     for count in range(len(discounts)):
21       if discountcode == discounts[count][0]:
22         discount = discounts[count][1]
23         valid = True
24
25     if valid == False:
26       print("Invalid discount code")
27
28   total = total - (total*discount)
29   print("Your total is £%.2f" %total)
30
```

CHALLENGE 45: STORE DISCOUNT CONTINUED...

Q1) Re-write the 2D list to include another discount code called "loyalty25" worth 25% off.

Q2) What is the data type of the variable `valid`?

Q3) Assume your 2D list in Q1 is now stored in a text file called "`codes.txt`". What would you need to write between lines 15-19 so that the discount codes are read from the text file?

Q4) The program could be re-written using subprograms. Explain the advantages of using subprograms i.e. procedures or functions.

CHALLENGE 46: BUBBLE SORT SNIPPET

A bubble sort iterates through an array (or list) of numbers from left to right. If the number being checked is greater than the next item in the array, the numbers are swapped. One way of achieving this is by storing the first number in a temporary vaiable.

Part of the bubble sort is shown below. j is a variable in a nested for loop which allows the algorithm to iterate over the length of the nums list.

```
1      nums = [9,1,12,3,4,8]
...
15     if nums[j] > nums[j+1] :
16         temp = nums[j]
17         nums[j] = nums[j+1]
18         nums[j+1] = nums[j]
19         swapped = True
```

The nums list can be visualised below:

nums[j]	nums[j+1]				
9	1	12	3	4	8

Q1) After the program runs, what is the value of temp?

Q2) In the above scenario, what are the final values of nums[j] and nums[j+1]? Explain whether the bubble sort has worked for the first two items?

CHALLENGE 46 BUBBLE SORT SNIPPET CONTINUED...

Q3) What is the name of the programming construct shown in the program:

A.   Sequence
B.   Selection
C.   Iteration

Q4) Give the name of two variables in the bubble sort snippet:

Q5) Name another sorting algorithm which might be more effective on a larger data set:

Q6) Explain why you might use a bubble sort instead of a different sorting algorithm:

CHALLENGE 47: CALCULATING THE FILE SIZE OF A TEXT FILE

The size of a text file can be calculated by using the following formula:

File size = bits per character * number of characters

Q1) Write a subprogram which takes the bits per character and number of characters as parameters and returns the file size in

Q2) ASCII is a character set which always uses 8 bits per character

If a text file encoded using ASCII has 1000 characters. How many bits will the file size be?

Q3) Text is always stored as binary. ASCII has 8 bits and therefore can represent 2^8 characters. Some formats of Unicode use 32 bits per character. This would create larger file sizes. Explain why

CHALLENGE 47: CALCULATING THE FILE SIZE OF A TEXT FILE CONTINUED...

Q4) The file size returned will be given in bits, therefore we can convert this to Kilobytes by dividing the answer by (8 * 1000.)

Use the space below to show how the function may be called. The answer should be outputted in KB.

Q5) Give your answer to Q2 from the previous page in Kilobytes:

CHALLENGE 48: CALCULATING THE FILE SIZE OF A SOUND FILE

The size of a sound file can be calculated by using the following formula:

File size = sample rate * bit depth * duration

Write a subprogram which takes the sample rate (a frequency measured in Hz), bit depth and duration (measured in seconds) of a sound file and returns the file size.

CHALLENGE 48: CALCULATING THE FILE SIZE OF A SOUND FILE CONTINUED...

The file size returned will be given in bits.

Use the space below to show how the function may be called. The answer should be outputted twice, once in KB and again in MB.

SOLUTIONS

Eirini Kolaiti came up with the great idea of putting example solutions to the challenges at the back of the book. I will also post these solutions online at: http://bit.do/LBOA2

There is always more than one way to solve a problem. Even if the algorithm is well-defined, there may be alternative programming approaches. The following pages present examples which you can compare to your own answers. Comments have been provided to aid your understanding, you should develop the habit of commenting all your programs.

Do not worry if you have written an alternative solution. Also be aware that these solutions were not produced by typing the whole program out and running them with no syntax and logic errors on the first time! There was a debugging process as I wrote each line or block of code. Encountering errors whilst iteratively testing is the "normal" way to develop programs.

CHALLENGES 1 AND 2:

```python
#define a function called highest_num with three parameters
def highest_number (num1, num2, num3):
    # return the highest number
    if num1 >= num2 and num1 >= num3:
        return num1
    elif num2 >= num1 and num2 >= num3:
        return num2
    else:
        return num3


first = int(input("Enter the first number: "))
second = int(input("Enter the second number: "))
third = int(input("Enter the third number: "))

#   call the highest_number function and pass the contents of
#   first, second and third variables as arguments into the
#   parameters num1, num2, num3
highest = highest_number(first,second,third)

#output the highest number with a meaningful message
print("The highest number is " + str(highest))
```

CHALLENGES 3 AND 4:

```
def options(num):
    if num == 1:
        return "Computer Science"
    elif num == 2:
        return "Music"
    elif num == 3:
        return "Dance"
    elif num == 4:
        return "PE"
    else:
        return "Error"

def main():
    print("""
1 Computer Science
2 Music
3 Dance
4 PE
    """)
    opt_num = int(input("Enter a number to choose an
option"))
    subject = options(opt_num)
    if subject == "Error":
        print("You entered an invalid number")
        print("Please enter a number between 1 and 4")
        return main()
    else:
        print("You chose", subject)
main()
```

CHALLENGE 5:

Q1)

num_in	Ouput
8	8
3	8
12	12
5	5

Q2) Lines 4-7

Q3) 3 is less than 5 so the first branch of the if statement is executed and the output is 8. The latter elif num == 3 branch is never reached.

CHALLENGE 6:

```
def mystery_number(num):
    if num == 3:
        print(1)
    elif num < 5:
        print(8)
    else:
        print(num)

num_in = int(input("Enter a number: "))
mystery_number(num_in)
```

CHALLENGE 7:

```
# B, E, D, C, A

def subtract(num1, num2):
    if num1 > num 2:
        out = num1 - num2
    else:
        out = num2 - num1
    return out

num1_in = int(input("Enter a number"))
num2_in = int(input("Enter a number"))

difference = subtract(num1_in, num2_in)
print("The difference is", difference)
```

CHALLENGE 8:

1) A. A function has parameters, a procedure does not
2) C. if num1 is greater than 9
3) C. Arguments
4) D. Def

CHALLENGE 9:

```
def initials_only(first, middle, last):
    #slice only the first character from each string
    initials = first[0]+middle[0]+last[0]

    return initials

firstname = input("What is your first name")
midname = input("What is your middle name")
lastname = input("What is your last name")

#call initials_only, passing the 3 names in as arguements
initials=initials_only(firstname,midname,lastname)

print("Your initials are:",initials)
```

CHALLENGE 10:

```
def subject_shortener(subject):
    shortened = subject[0:3]

    return shortened

subj = input("Enter the subject name")

subj_out=subject_shortener(subj)

print(subj,"has been shortened to",subj_out)

def cuboid_volume (length, width, height):
    volume = length * width * height

    return volume
```

CHALLENGE 11:

```
length_in = int(input("Enter the length of the cuboid: "))
width_in = int(input("Enter the width of the cuboid: "))
height_in = int(input("Enter the height of the cuboid: "))

volume_out = cuboid_volume(length_in, width_in, height_in)
print("The volume of the cuboid is " + str(volume_out))
```

CHALLENGE 12:

```
def add(num1, num2):
    out = num1 + num2
    return out

num1_in = int(input("Enter a number"))
num2_in = int(input("Enter a number"))

total = add(num1_in, num2_in)

print("The sum is", total)
```

CHALLENGE 13:

1) C. na
2) B. o
3) D. 8
4) B. A value which can not change whilst the program is running

CHALLENGE 14:

```
def is_odd(number_in):
    if int(number_in) %2 == 0:
        return("The number is even")
    else:
        return("The number is odd")


def main():
    number = input("Enter a number")

    if number != "STOP" :
        odd = is_odd(number)
        print(odd)
        # call the main function again i.e. loop back to the
top
        # and ask for another number
        return main()
    else:
        exit()

#Always run main() first unless the program is imported
if __name__ == '__main__':
    main()
```

CHALLENGE 15:

```
def is_multiple(x_in, y_in):
    if x_in % y_in == 0:
        print(x_in, "is  a multiple of", y_in)
    else:
        print(x_in, "is not a multiple of", y_in)

print("A program to check if x is a multiple of y")
x = int(input("Enter a number to check if it is a multiple"))
y = int(input("Enter a number to divide by"))

#Call the procedure, passing in x and y
is_multiple(x,y)
```

CHALLENGE 16:

Q1)

num1	num2	Output
1	8	0
3	9	1
14	10	2
21	19-28	4

Q2)

a) 21 DIV 7 = 3

b) 9 DIV 4 = 2

c) 8 DIV 3 = 2

CHALLENGE 17:

```
sentinel = "XXX" #The sentinel value
word = ""
acronym = ""
while word != sentinel: #could also replace sentinel with
"XXX"
  word = input("Enter a word or \"XXX\" to finish")
  if word != sentinel:
    acronym = acronym + word[0]

print(acronym)
```

CHALLENGE 18:

```
acronym = ""
words = input("Enter words to be turned into an
acronym")

#Convert the words sentence into a list words, separated
by commas
words_list = words.split()

#For each word in the words string
#Same as for count in range(len(words)):
for word in words_list:
    acronym = acronym + word[0]
print(acronym)
```

CHALLENGE 19:

```
import random

#   initialise the dice with two different values so the
#   program runs at least once
dice1 = 1
dice2 = 2

while dice1 != dice2:
    dice1 = random.randint(1,6)
    dice2 = random.randint(1,6)

    print("Dice 1 rolled:" + str(dice1))
    print("Dice 2 rolled:" + str(dice2))

    if dice1 == dice2:
        print("Game loading")
    else:
        # Use input to enable the user to press enter to continue
        #  looping
        again = input("Press enter to roll again")
```

CHALLENGE 20:

```
import random

#  initialise the score with a value of 0
score = 0

for count in range(3):
    dice1 = random.randint(1,6)
    dice2 = random.randint(1,6)

    print("Dice 1 rolled:" + str(dice1))
    print("Dice 2 rolled:" + str(dice2))

    total = dice1 + dice2
    print("Your total for this round is:",total)

    score = score + total
    print("Your running score is now:", score)

print("Your final score after 3 rounds is:", score)
```

CHALLENGE 21:

```
numbers = [9, 8, 72, 22, 21, 81, 2, 1, 11, 76, 32, 54]

highest = numbers[0]

for count in range(len(numbers)):
   if highest < numbers[count]:
      highest = numbers[count]

print("The highest number is", highest)
```

CHALLENGE 22:

```
numbers = [9, 8, 72, 22, 21, 81, 2, 1, 11, 76, 32, 54]

def highest_num(numbers_in):
    highest = numbers[0]

    for count in range(len(numbers)):
        if highest < numbers[count]:
            highest = numbers[count]

    return highest

highest_out = highest_num(numbers)
print("The highest number is", highest_out)
```

CHALLENGES 23 AND 24:

```
obvious = ["password", "qwerty", "hello123", "letmein", "123456"]

password = input("Please enter a password: ")

#  A basic linear search which iterates through the obvious
#  list to check for matches against the password
for count in range(len(obvious)):
    if password == obvious[count]:
        print("This password is weak. It uses a common word or \
phrase making it susceptible to a brute force attack")

#  Length check
if len(password) < 8:
    print("Your password is too short. Please use at least \
8 characters")

#  initialise some counter variables for different types of
#  characters
char = 0
num = 0
upper = 0
lower = 0

for count in range(len(password)):
    #  A linear search to check if the character is a digit
    if password[count].isdigit():
        num = num+1
    #  A check to see if the character is an upper or lower char
    elif password[count].isalpha():
        char = char+1
        if password[count].isupper():
            upper = upper+1
        elif password[count].islower():
            lower = lower+1

if num == 0:
    print("To make your password more secure, you could include \
numbers")
if upper == 0 or lower ==0:
    print("To make your password more secure, you could include \
upper and lower case letters")
if char == 0:
    print("To make your password more secure, you could include \
letters")
if num > 0 and char > 0 and upper > 0 and lower > 0:
    print("Your password meets the minimum length requirements \
and contains a mixture of numbers, characters, upper and lower
case letters.")
```

CHALLENGE 25:

```
import random

keeper = ["left", "centre", "right"]

keeper_score = 0
player_score = 0
for count in range(5):
    dive = random.choice(keeper)

    player = input("Do you wish to shoot to the left, centre or
right: ")

    print("Keeper went to the", dive)

    if keeper == player:
        print("Penalty saved")
        keeper_score = keeper_score+1
    else:
        print("GOAAAAAAL!")
        player_score = player_score+1

if keeper_score > player_score:
    print("Keeper wins", keeper_score, "-", player_score)
else:
    print("You win!", player_score, "-", keeper_score)
```

CHALLENGE 26:

1)

x	y
0	2
1	2
2	4
3	4

2) `for x in range (1,11)`

3) It initialises the variable y to a value of 0 so that it can be used later in the for loop.

CHALLENGE 27:

Circle the correct answer based on the following code:

```
import random
for count in range(0,5):
  num1=random.randint(1,10)
```

1) A. 10 and 1
2) B. 0 and 4
3) A. 5 times

4) for words in sentence
or for count in range(0,5)
or for count in range(len(sentence))

CHALLENGE 28:

```
def mean_of_list(numbers_list_in):
   total = 0
   for count in range(len(numbers_list_in)):
      total = total + numbers_list_in[count]

   #  divide by the length of the list to find the mean
   average = total / len(numbers_list_in)
   return average


def main():
   numbers_list = [0,7,5,3,22,23,11,34,51,32,5,3,1]

   mean = mean_of_list(numbers_list)
   print("The mean average of", numbers_list, "=", mean)


main()

#  A better way to call main in case the file is imported:
#  if __name__ == '__main__':
#       main()
```

CHALLENGE 29:

```python
def vowel_counter(sentence):
    A = 0
    E = 0
    I = 0
    O = 0
    U = 0

    for count in range(len(sentence)):
        #  The .upper() casts the current letter to an upper
case
        #  Without .uppper(), we would write
        #  if sentence[count] == "A" or sentence[count] ==
"a":
        if sentence[count].upper() == "A":
            A = A+1
        elif sentence[count].upper() == "E":
            E = E+1
        elif sentence[count].upper() == "I":
            I = I+1
        elif sentence[count].upper() == "O":
            O =O+1
        elif sentence [count].upper() == "U":
            U = U+1

    #  using comma to concatenate in Python means we can cast
    #  the integer values implicitly without using str()
    print("The number of A's:", A)
    print("The number of E's:", E)
    print("The number of I's:", I)
    print("The number of O's:", O)
    print("The number of U's:", U)


sentence = "Learning programming is similar to learning a
musical instrument. Both involve practise and making lots of
mistakes. Both also require perseverence to develop fluency.
Keep going!"

vowel_counter(sentence)
```

CHALLENGE 30:

```
def marks(grade_in):
    grades = [["A*","90"],["A","83"],["B","72"],
              ["C","60"],["D","49"],["E","30"]]

    for count in range(len(grades)):
        if grades[count][0] == grade_in:
            return grades[count][1]


grade = input("What grade do you wish to achieve: ")
mark_req = marks(grade)
print("For grade", grade, "you need to gain", mark_req)
```

CHALLENGE 31 SOLUTION 1:

```
def vowel_counter(sentence):
    vowel_list=[ ["A",0],
                 ["E",0],
                 ["I",0],
                 ["O",0],
                 ["U",0]]

    for count in range(len(sentence)):
        #  The .upper() casts the current letter to an upper
case
        #  Without .uppper(), we would write
        #  if sentence[count] == "A" or sentence[count] == "a":
        if sentence[count].upper() == "A":
            vowel_list[0][1] = (vowel_list[0][1])+1
        elif sentence[count].upper() == "E":
            vowel_list[1][1] = (vowel_list[1][1])+1
        elif sentence[count].upper() == "I":
            vowel_list[2][1] = (vowel_list[2][1])+1
        elif sentence[count].upper() == "O":
            vowel_list[3][1] = (vowel_list[3][1])+1
        elif sentence [count].upper() == "U":
            vowel_list[4][1] = (vowel_list[4][1])+1

    #  using comma to concatenate in Python means we can cast
    #  the integer values implicitly without using str()
    print("The number of A's:", vowel_list[0][1])
    print("The number of E's:", vowel_list[1][1])
    print("The number of I's:", vowel_list[2][1])
    print("The number of O's:", vowel_list[3][1])
    print("The number of U's:", vowel_list[4][1])


sentence = "Learning programming is similar to learning a
musical instrument. Both involve practice and making lots of
mistakes. Both also require perseverence to develop fluency.
Keep going!"

vowel_counter(sentence)
```

CHALLENGE 31 SOLUTION 2 NESTED FOR LOOP:

```
def vowel_counter(sentence):
    vowel_list=[ ["A",0],
                 ["E",0],
                 ["I",0],
                 ["O",0],
                 ["U",0]]

    #for each character
    for count in range(len(sentence)):
      #for each vowel in the vowel_list
      for letter in range(len(vowel_list)):
          #if the character == vowel
          if sentence[count].upper() == vowel_list[letter][0]:
              #increment that vowel's counter
              vowel_list[letter][1] = (vowel_list[letter][1])+1

 #loop through each vowel in vowel_list and output their totals
    for vowels in range(len(vowel_list)):
       print("The number of",vowel_list[vowels][0],\
"is",vowel_list[vowels][1])


sentence = "Learning programming is similar to learning a
musical instrument. Both involve practice and making lots of
mistakes. Both also require perseverence to develop fluency.
Keep going!"

vowel_counter(sentence)
```

CHALLENGE 32:

```
cs_scores = [["Karman","45","60","72"],
             ["Daniel","55","65","70"],
             ["Parker","71","78","78"],
             ["Jessica","68","79","80"],
             ["Edie","98","85","91"]]

total = 0

for exam in range(1,4):
#  iterate through each exam
    for student in range(len(cs_scores)):
    #  update the total by iterating through each student
        total = total + int(cs_scores[student][exam])

    #  calculate the total
    print("Total for exam num", exam, "=", total)
    #  reset the total before starting on the next exam
    total = 0
```

CHALLENGE 33:

```
cs_scores=[["Theo","45","60","72"],["Angharad","55","65","70"],
           ["Sameer","71","78","78"],"Adrian","68","79","80"],
           ["Ayana","98","85","91"]]

total = 0

for exam in range(1,4):
#  iterate through each exam
    for student in range(len(cs_scores)):
    #  update the total by iterating through each student
    total = total + int(cs_scores[student][exam])

    #  calculate and output the mean
    mean = total / len(cs_scores)
    print("Mean average for exam num", exam, "=", mean)

    #  reset the total before starting on the next exam
    total = 0
```

CHALLENGE 34:

```
cs_scores=[["Theo","45","60","72"],["Angharad","55","65","70"],
          ["Sameer","71","78","78"],"Adrian","68","79","80"],
          ["Ayana","98","85","91"]]

def mean_student(scores_in):
    total = 0

    for exam in range(1,4):
    #   iterate through each exam
        for student in range(len(cs_scores)):
        #   update the total by iterating through each student
            total = total + int(cs_scores[student][exam])

        #   calculate and output the mean
        mean = total / len(cs_scores)
        print("Mean average for exam num", exam, "=", mean)

        #   reset the total before starting on the next exam
        total = 0

mean_student(cs_scores)
```

CHALLENGE 35:

1)

x	y	output
0	0	Charlie
0	1	Dog
0	2	8
1	0	Dolly
1	1	Sheep

2) 2D-List
3) C. Iteration

CHALLENGE 36:

1) B 2,3,4,5,3,4,5,6,3,4,5,6
2) C Wanda
3) D Index error: list index out of range

CHALLENGES 37 AND 38:

```
def generate_username (firstname, lastname):
    #  create username based on the lastname and first intiial
    username = lastname + firstname[0]

    #  open the file in read mode and evaluate its contents
    users_file = open("users.txt","r")
    usernames = eval(users_file.read())
    users_file.close()

    #  check the entire 2D array to see if the username exists
    for count in range(len(usernames)):
        #  if the username exists, add a # symbol
        if usernames[count][0] == username:
            username = username + "#"

    #  return the final username
    return username


forename = input("Enter your first name: ")
surname = input("Enter your surname: ")

username_out = generate_username(forename, surname)
```

CHALLENGE 39:

```
def new_user(username_in, password_in):
    # define a function called new_user with two parameters:
    # username and password

    users_file = open("users.txt", "r")  # open file in read mode

    users = eval(users_file.read())       # use eval to read in the
                                          # 2D list

    users_file.close()                    # close the file

    new_user = []                         # make a new list for the
                                          # new user
    new_user.append(username_in)          # append the username to
                                          # the new user list

    new_user.append(password_in)          # append the password to
                                          # the same list

    # ppend new user list to existing 2D list that we read in
    users.append(new_user)

    users_file = open("users.txt", "w")  # open file in write mode

    # cast updated 2D list as a string and write string to the file
    users_file.write(str(users))

    users_file.close()                    #   close the file
print("Your username is " + str(username_out))
```

CHALLENGE 40

1) B
file = open("txtfile.txt", "a")
file.write("some text")

2) A Allow you to write to a file, wiping the original data

3) A Close the file

CHALLENGE 41

B
```
email = input ("Enter a username")
```

A
```
file = open ("users.txt","r")

users = eval(file.read())
```

C
```
file.close()
```

G
```
found = False
```

D
```
for count in range(len(users)):
```

F
```
    if email == users[count][0]:
        found = True
        return Found
```

E
```
return Found
```

Correct order:

B	A	C	G	D	F	E

CHALLENGE 42

```
def hex_to_denary(hex_in):
    # only convert values A to F
    hex_A_to_F = [["A","10"],["B","11"],["C","12"],["D","13"],
["E","14"],["F","15"]]

    convert = False
    for count in range(len(hex_A_to_F)):
        if hex_in == hex_A_to_F[count][0]:
            convert = True
            return int(hex_A_to_F[count][1])

    # if values are not A-F i.e. 1-9, return these as integers
    if convert == False:
        return int(hex_in)

def main():

    hexi = input("Enter a hex digit to convert: ")
    hex_out = hex_to_denary(hexi)
    print("The denary equivalent is", hex_out)


main()

# A better way to call main in case the file is imported:
# if __name__ == '__main__':
#     main()
```

CHALLENGE 43

1) A

2) quiz() procedure has not been called

3) Declare a variable called score and initialise it to 0 so that we can keep track of the score by passing it into the correct procedure on line 25

110

CHALLENGE 44

1) 30

2) List or Array

3) 2

4) Element is present at index 3

5) Element is not present in array

6) Integer division or floor division. A division where you ignore the remainder and round down.

7) integer

CHALLENGE 45

1)
```
discounts = [["summer10",0.1],
             ["welcome",0.15],
             ["refer20",0.2],
             ["loyalty25",0.25]]
```

2) Boolean

3)
```
file = open("codes.txt","r")
discounts = eval(file.read())
file.close()
```

4)

- Subprograms such as procedures and functions can be called anywhere in the program.
- Subprograms reduce the number of lines of code i.e. creates shorter programs.
- The programs are also more manageable as errors or changes to one subprogram means you only make the change or the correction in one place, not several places throughout the program.

4 continued)

- Multiple people can work on the program, each working on a different subprogram.
- The subprograms can be tested in isolation.
- Subprograms can be re-used in other programs and also imported .

CHALLENGE 46

1) Based on the snippet shown, nums[j] is 9 and this is stored in temp.

2) nums[j] and nums[j+1] both equal 1. The bubble sort has not worked. Line 18 should be nums[j+1] = temp. This ensures the original value of nums[j] i.e. 9 is stored in temp and then copied to nums[j]. The code as it stands first replaces nums[j] with 1 then replaces the value of nums[j+1] with the updated value of nums[j].

3) Selection

4) Any two from: temp, j and swapped

5) Insertion sort or merge sort

6) It uses little memory and is not processor intensive. If the array to be sorted is short or mostly already sorted, a bubble sort will be quicker to program and potentially quicker to run than an insertion sort or merge sort. These other sorting algorithms scal better i.e. they are suited for larger data sets,

CHALLENGE 47

1)
```
def text_size(bits_char, num_char):
    size = bits_char * num_char
    return size
```

2) 8 * 1000 = 8000 bits

3) More characters can be represented (2^{32}) in Unicode. Unicode includes emojis and non-English characters such as Japanese and Chinese.

4)
```
def main():

    bits = int(input("Enter the number of bits per character: "))
    charact = int(input("Enter the number of characters: "))

    size_out = file_size(bits, charact)
    size_kb = size_out / (8 * 1000)

    print("The file size is", size_kb, "KB")


#A better way to call main in case the file is imported:
if __name__ == '__main__':
    main()
```

5) 1KB

CHALLENGE 48

```
def file_size(frequency, bits, duration):
  size = frequency * bits *  duration
  return size

def main():

  freq = int(input("Enter the frequency in Hz: "))
  bit_depth = int(input("Enter the bit depth: "))
  length = int(input("Enter the duration of the sound file in \
seconds: "))

  size_out = file_size(freq, bit_depth, length)
  size_kb = size_out / (8 * 1000)
  size_mb = size_kb / 1000
  print("The file size is", size_kb, "KB")
  print("The file size is", size_mb, "MB")


#A better way to call main in case the file is imported:
if __name__ == '__main__':
    main()
```

FURTHER READING

FOR STUDENTS AND TEACHERS:

Coding Club Python Basics Level 1 (2012) [1]   Chris Roffey
Coding Club Next Steps Level 2 (2013)

Python by Example[1]   Nichola Lacey

Making Games with Python and Pygame (2012)   Al Sweigart
Automate The Boring Stuff With Python (2015)
www.inventwithpython.com

www.pythonprogramming.net   Sentdex
See also: Youtube channel- sentdex

www.kidscancode.org   Chris and Priya
See also: Youtube channel- KidsCanCode   Bradfield

Youtube channel- MrLauLearning   William Lau

Youtube channel- Tech With Tim   Tech With Tim

Youtube channel- Corey Schafer   Corey Schafer

Youtube channel- Computerphile   Computerphile

How We Learn (2014)   Benedict Carey

Why We Sleep (2017)   Matthew Walker

FOR TEACHERS:

Teaching Computing in Secondary Schools   William Lau

Computer Science Education   Edited by Sue Sentance,
     Erik Barendsen and
     Carsten Schulte

Teach Like a Champion 2.0   Doug Lemov

Tools for Teaching   Fred Jones

[1] Brilliant books for absolute beginners. These "how-to" guides take you step by step through the basic programming structures required to access most of the material in this book.

ACKNOWLEDGEMENTS

My knowledge and understanding of programming was initially developed by attending courses run by Ilia Avroutine, Darren Travi, Graham Bradshaw, David Batty and Sarah Shakibi. I have also benefitted greatly from the mentoring of Merijn Broeren, Elizabeth Hidson and Andy Swann.

The generosity of those who produce resources to teach programming such as Chris Roffey, Al Sweigart and Sentdex along with the wider CAS and Facebook community is also a great source of inspiration. To all of the aforementioned, I am indebted. You have given me the confidence to keep developing my programming skills independently and to eventually share these skills with you on CAS, Facebook, Youtube and in my books.

To further my understanding of programming, I have had the great privilege of sharing thoughts with Peter Kemp, Alex Parry, Eirini Kolaiti, Richard Pawson, Scott Portnoff, Sue Sentence, Meg Ray and Alan Harrison. All of the brilliant teachers and programmers read drafts of this book and their comments have improved the book significantly.

I hope that my compromise of including procedures as well as non-modular programs is forgiven. I have to be realistic and acknowledge that for all novices, writing programs without subroutines is a starting point and an achievement in itself. There are many solutions to a given algorithm and provided that the output is correct and the algorithm is reasonably efficient, we should recognise these as correct (up to GCSE level) even if subroutines are not used.

I thank my colleagues, particularly Lloyd Stevens, Leila Lassami, Jaime Vega, Gavin Tong, Sahima Patel, John Seery, Agata Obirek and Jamie Brownhill at Central Foundation Boys' School (CFBS). They have supported me with their time, patience and agreeable responses to my (occasionally unreasonable) demands! I also thank the students at CFBS whose hard work have provided me with further motivation to improve my teaching . Our students always inspire us to be better .

To Suki, Zi and Q, this book would not be possible without you. Many people ask me how I have time to write these books and my answer is, "I have an understanding family!" Thank you for your continued support.

SPACE FOR FURTHER PRACTISE AND NOTES

Printed in Great Britain
by Amazon

14614379R00071